Silent Suffering

Silent Suffering

Poems of Pain & Purpose

LESLIE CORBLY

Foreword by KEITH ADAMS

RESOURCE *Publications* · Eugene, Oregon

SILENT SUFFERING
Poems of Pain and Purpose

Resource Publications
An Imprint of Wipf and Stock Publishers
199 W. 8th Ave., Suite 3
Eugene, OR 97401

www.wipfandstock.com

PAPERBACK ISBN: 979-8-3852-0554-7
HARDCOVER ISBN: 979-8-3852-0555-4
EBOOK ISBN: 979-8-3852-0556-1

Acknowledgements

Written for those under progressive oppression
May you find courage, your stoic silence to break
Irreverently ask and answer all questions
For when truth is spoken, evil you will forsake

Contents

Contents

Foreword

Leslie Corbly's poetry offers a remarkable journey into unvarnished vulnerability. This journey is shaped by a fiercely intelligent exhortation to examine the status quo. She asks many *whys*. She dares to engage the origins and resulting tributaries of churning cultural undercurrents with cleverness and specificity. Leslie Corbly is a breath of fresh air.

Poetry is an expression having roots that extend back over 4,000 years. The earliest forms of the oral tradition of poetic storytelling have been integral to the sharing of ideas, values, cultural practices, wisdom, and knowledge for centuries before the art was introduced in written form. Poetry has taken many forms and expressions throughout human history. That being true, poetry has and continues to serve us well in illuminating the arc of human experience.

Poetry is more than the communication of raw data or information. Poetry is a purposed revelatory expression that evokes, disturbs, and illuminates brokenness and beauty while inviting the reader or listener with a posture of honest and vulnerable reflection. It is a literary genre that is filled with shaded nuance and that embraces multiple dimensions. Every nuance and dimension matters. Words are chosen by the poet just as Van Gogh, Rembrandt, or Rothko selected color, form, and stroke in bringing to life visual wonder on a canvas. Poetry gives attention to the meaning of a word, while meticulously considering how the word sounds or looks, its lilting or jagged rhythm, the number of syllables, or the emotive sense a word may stir.

Poetry is a unique kind of experience.

In the 2009 movie *Bright Star*, based on the tragically short life of poet John Keats, a particular scene portrayed the budding curiosity of Fanny Brawne regarding the meaning and understanding of poetry. Fanny confesses to Keats, "I still don't know how to work out a poem." Keats responds,

> A poem needs understanding through the senses. The point of diving in a lake is not immediately to swim to the shore, but to be in the lake, to luxuriate in the sensation of water. You do not work the lake out. It is an experience beyond thought. Poetry soothes and emboldens the soul to accept mystery.

Clearly, this response—attributed to Keats in exploring poetic nuance—is not dismissing intellect. Rather it is an invitation to a broader awareness of how we "experience" the poetic art form more holistically and completely to immerse readers and listeners into the rawness of humanity.

Leslie Corbly offers a provocative work. She respectfully guides her readers to engage this work and our world holistically. She invites her readers to reflect honestly and boldly. She is incisive and courageous. Her poetic expressions address a wide range of issues with piercing curiosity. She artfully illuminates crevices in current cultural decorum, and then challenges readers to explore beneath the surface offerings of seemingly arbitrary societal expectations.

Leslie Corbly's approach is refreshingly unapologetic. She can be irreverent. To some, she might be shocking. However, she is never flippant nor cheap. She brings thoughtful passion to bear at every turn. She cares deeply and invites her readers to care as well. Her work also has depth and gravitas. Her purposeful immersion in both current and historic works of respected masters in the fields of literature, philosophy and theology can be clearly seen as significant influences for her, and for her reflections.

A hopeful ache and inspiring creativity pulses in each syllable of Leslie Corbly's poetry. It cuts, provokes, and invites. She nudges us—at times not so gently—to pay attention and consider asking deeper questions about what is really happening in and around us.

Keith Adams, BM, MATS
Redeeming Life, Founder
Oklahoma City, OK

YEARNINGS

INTIMACY

Elusive to define
Easy from its grasp to flee
True intimacy is sublime
But never known for free

It can be the sword of the unjust
For another's heart can never be known
Predicated upon foundations of trust
Who stands before you through time is shown

It is safer to stand alone
Is the pain worth the risk?
But in isolation there is no shalom
Fear, hope, hate, love, all feelings are mixed

What metric can be used
To filter wheat from chaff?
To ensure the soul is not abused
By those who turn hope to ash?

Care must ever be taken
To distinguish between
Those who awaken
Deep, yet irrational dreams

For those who seek
Intimacy in its purest form
Love is ultimately worth the fire
Through which relationships are born

MISSING MEANING

Lace, Dolce, Gucci, Wine
Nothing out of place
Her life was sublime

Days full of bliss
No distress in sight
Is this not happiness?

Relationships full of care
Security surrounds her
There is no cause for fear

Yet from the loneliness she runs
A stranger to internal peace
For no earthly paradise
Can put her mind at ease

AWARENESS

His broken phone brought solitude
Now his mind had nowhere to go
The vastness of the open world
Made time stand still, all felt . . . slow

Seconds later his mind flinched
What was that inside his ear?
He looked around the room
Unsure of what it was he feared

He noticed the silence had a sound
Why was this making his head pound?
Why did he feel as if he had drowned?

As the silence grew his pain increased
What was the cause of this distress?
Just yesterday had felt like bliss
Now inside he was a mess

AVOIDANCE

Fleeing from deep pain
Comes at a terrible price
From thinking one must abstain
Making the mind unwise

As the asset of time passes by
Interest only increases
Even when you want to try
Compounded pain the mind does freeze

Avoiding pain in youth
Only stunts development
Instead of learning to improve
Awareness brings embitterment

DISAPPEAR

Tired, lonely, drenched in sorrow
Full of fear, a partaker in life's pain
Unable to see hope in tomorrow
Waves of torment, am I insane?

Time fades on, the world is unchanged
Green grass still blows in the wind
My spirit remains internally untamed
Tormented, my being begs for life to end

My body releases one heavy sigh
What does one make of internal derision?
Externally still, yet internally crying
My mind concocts deathly visions

The blue skies turned to a fiery red
Hope burned in the ash of a deathbed
The taste of anger gave way to rest
As life disappeared into glorious death

DESPAIR

A crushing sense of pain
An endless internal fight
Drives the wise insane
A life of eternal strife

Deep in the darkness
Despair appears to cure
The perpetual loneliness
From which escape is unsure

Why hold onto hope?
Is it not fool's gold?
Blind and weary, I grope
Drowning, there is nothing to hold

Day by day despair
Whispers, calling my name
Slowly fades the desire to care
For the outcome of life's cruel game

DESIRES

Confusing, often contradictory
From these loose fragments
Emerges one complete story

Days are disconnected
Disembodied one from the other
Internal states must be dissected

Fleeting emotions speak powerfully
Anger, hatred, and death press on my mind
from my desires, will I ever be free?

Yet some are for good
Seeking truth and beauty
Hungry for spiritual food

Discerning between these desires
Some noble, others evil
Wisdom must come from higher

Alone, desires are all my eye can see
Seductively, they overwhelm my mind
The truth must come from outside of me

COMING TO BELIEF

Once life was simple
Free from emotive desires
Without a sacred temple,
Nothing in humanity to admire

Simplicity was shattered
Truth clearly showed
Care for earthly matters
I can no longer stand alone

Time moves like sinking sand
The weight of divine command
Lays heavy on the mind of one
Who prefers alone to stand

Isolated, apart from the world's
Earthly, external form
This new reality, I mourned
And human attachment I scorned

What of the commands of God?
Why must He speak to me?
I was content to walk alone
But will not deny what my mind sees

The fright runs deep
This earth is surely cursed,
Moving forward, I weep
Feeling lonely and coerced

Trapped in a world I long to subvert
Instead I am told to belong
With humans, less worthy than dirt
Yet God calls me to sing *His* song

THE SPIRIT SPEAKS

Following rules can avoid pain
But legality cannot explain
How to live a good life
Obedience alone is in vain

Law can keep order
But it does not inspire
Preventing harm
Does not create the Shire

A world of possibilities
Means harm may occur
The law can be broken
Nothing can be assured

Within a world of chaos
Order must be brought
But rules cannot suffice
The spirit must be sought

THE SPIRIT SUFFERS

Who am I?
The question makes you cry
For it is not clear how to know
What defines who you are inside

Am I flesh or blood?
Is there more to my being?
Do I have a spirit?
Or am I contriving what I am seeing?

Before I conceived of this spirit
My mind was full of clutter
Now inside, fear resides
Must this spirit make me suffer?

THE SPIRIT SUSTAINS

Knowing right from wrong
Creates a unique tension
Between a desire to belong
And the inner disposition

My spirit may conflict
With messages around me
I cannot be perfect
For truth is hard to see

What can bring me aid
In my time of need?
My spirit is often broken
Does one within sanctify me?

HOPE

Is it by habit or design,
The breath you breathe?
Is your life yours
Or merely a physical sign
Of what the world sees?

Why live without a voice
Describing your beliefs?
Hope is not easy, it is a choice
That need not end with relief

Hope is no empty cliché
Spoken to retain worldly peace
Hope sees past earthly decay
Even as pain may increase

EUDAIMONIA

Eudaimonia, Greek for flourish
A state humanity strives to experience
Still, its conditions are hard to nourish
Demanding high emotive rents

What does it mean to flourish?
Is it a life free of pain?
How can this be when humanity
Struggles to stay sane?

Indeed, the Greeks felt deep pain
They lived with many a vice
Yet many were more sane
Than modern men who spur their advice

Ancient wisdom may sound odd
To the modern ear
We write it off as deeply flawed
And instead live in fear

SATISFACTION

External circumstances change
And happiness is fleeting
In this world we feel estranged
Searching for eternal meaning

A hopeless task for weak men
And women fare no better
Our minds are brittle; prone to sin
We are all moral debtors

We seek to change the world
For it is easier to believe
Ourselves as heroes of the good
Than those in desperate need

Yet utopias have always failed
For life on earth is hard
In truth serenity prevails
In the minds of those who fear no scars
And understand earth is no heaven

AFTER LIFE

We suffer now, slaves to sin
Seeking swift pleasures
Unable to find peace within

We long for our nature to change
For an ending to strife
For this nightmare to end
And give birth to true life

INFINITE COMPLEXITY

WHAT IS GOOD?

People are good
Or is this true?
Do they act as they should?

These questions plague the open mind
What is loving, good, and kind?
Who ultimately decides?

What makes those traits good?
This question leaves all confused
For it is often not considered
How to determine what was true

Confusion compounds
As the mind expands
What standard determines good?
The honest find it hard to understand

Social expectations often rule our minds
For we do not like to be called unkind

The sands of time dictate perceptions
Of whether our actions appease
The gods of worldly deception
Who inject our minds with popular disease

Our desire for approval breeds self-deception
Calling us to act before we have thought
New ideas or concepts we readily reject
Afraid of being cast out, left emotionally distraught

Hateful! Bigot! Intolerant! Unkind!
These slurs serve a useful purpose
They control the collective mind

Keeping humanity within social service
Unable to think freely and unencumbered
In this prison thought can only scratch the surface

How can we exit this cage? Is there no way out?
Think for yourself, make room for doubt

Perhaps you are wrong about goodness
Maybe you are unable to see
Goodness and truth cannot be known
Without riding waves of deep uncertainty

TIMELESS DISPUTES

Foundational questions plague our minds
Easy to ask, but difficult to answer
Ignoring them makes us blind
Once resolved they are life's anchor

The basis of rational thought is forever being sought
No serious answer results in harmony
Paradoxically, predicates defy such certainty

Instead, foundations rest on faith
Making theory scary and safe
Each of us rests in abstract reality
Yet remain fearful when others disagree

One truth should give us comfort and rest
No one . . . not even earth's greatest minds
Are capable of full knowledge to assess
To some extent we all wonder blind

We all confront questions we do not understand
With aspects of truth we grapple and contend
Our answers we must know and defend
Even if our stances bristle and offend

For life is brief and knowledge limited
Absolute truth is real . . . absolute certainty is not
And so we must defend principles
Even with our limited, incomplete thought

Foundational thought is nothing novel
Each generation wrestles anew
Answers are necessary for human survival
All of us these timeless disputes pursue

Nature & Nurture

From birth to death some traits are innate
But the environment where humanity grows
Is a factor in determining human fate
Which is more important? No one really knows

Assuming nature creates your destiny
Gives rise to a dangerous apathy
Yet if environment is solely culpable
Then humanity becomes infinitely malleable

Why does the debate between nature and nurture rage on?
What makes it hard to turn away from this concern?

Concerning this question, we continue to discuss
For both ends of the spectrum can cause us to suffer
Reducing human life to genetic code causes disgust
Denying innate traits grants tyrants the right our will to smother

Believing life immutable and fixed is a type of mental prison
It keeps the mind from finding ways to break perverse patterns
At first glance learning of nurture seems to give man a clear
   mission

The plasticity of man means his life can be perfectly arranged
To optimize humanity's goodness, comfort, and pleasure
This may sound freeing, but it leads to the bondage of chains

In truth no one can fully determine their condition
Factors beyond mortal control eternally occur
Still we are not eased of our earthly mission
Justice and goodness we must move toward

Freedom & Virtue

Freedom and virtue are seen as contrary one to the other
The free man is not safe while the conformist lives in comfort
But this false dichotomy gives deceit a cover
Allowing us to live in fear and truth to distort

True freedom is not boundless impossibilities
There is no such thing as infinite choices
Few men exist outside of society
And those that do possess a passive voice

Boundaryless experience is merely an illusion
The tenet of faith for those dedicated to inclusion
Man's natural state is social and collective
Actions causing destruction are an unnatural objective

Why do we fear freedom if safety it does not condemn?
Because our nature is dual and full of mystery
We seek freedom our limits to transcend
This truth is undeniable, passed down through time and history

Properly understood, freedom requires virtue
But as is common with modern minds
Goodness has been twisted, endlessly devalued
True freedom is now hard to find

Liberty has been cheapened to a common price
Anyone can afford to cry for fictitious rights
The freedom on which the West traditionally rested
Served as a firm foundation for it was tried and tested

Rights and responsibilities should always run together
Each doing as they please at scale is a disaster

Instead of seeking the ability to live without interference
Freedom has been reborn to a perverse definition
Liberty loses its sense of internal coherence
When rights are invented and enforced on a whim

Rights themselves are few in number
They cannot be created out of thin air
Liberty is structural, tyranny to encumber
Emotional harm freedom cannot hope to repair

All want to partake in liberty's spoils
Few are willing culture to cultivate
Independence grows not in every soil
Freedom requires responsibility not be abdicated

Material Reality

The world is all there is, nothing exists beyond the physical
Of immaterial reality, the modern mind is critical
It is an odd proposition from those wedded to rationalism
For it is not possible to falsify this faith's central axiom

The material exists for all to see
Except those deemed untethered to reality

This presents an odd predicament
Imagine entering the mad man's mind
If he cannot define the physical
How would you convince him he was blind?

Axiomatic statements define internal realities
Still there is no ultimate guarantee
That something beyond our five senses
Has not been buried by mental defenses

Immaterial reality surrounds us all
Existing within every human connection
Why does love leave us enthralled?
No one claims affection is merely projection

The physical domain is impossible to deny
Some find comfort in restricting reality
Determined within a formula all truth to classify
Unable to wander through abstract lines of inquiry

Battles between the material and the spiritual
Are unlikely ever to truly abate
There is much ambiguity in the metaphysical
Still some will always prefer to limit the debate

To some the immaterial cannot exist
Science demands all reality is physical
Immaterialism is an illusion – a mental trick
This circular logic is accepted as typical

Still concepts define the physical cage
Character, compassion, and conceptual thought
Lose their meaning in a purely material age

After defining away the most important elements of the human
 condition
We loudly cry, wondering why society is riddled by suicide and
 addiction

The physical world is all we can see
Making some blind to fundamental elements of reality
Denial of truth always comes at a price
In a soulless era many lose their life

Truth & Desire

Truth and desire are notoriously easy to confuse
Desires are strong, pushing on all forms of our being
Strong feelings make truth easy to abuse
Often discarding truth will bring a sense of freedom

Desires themselves cannot be eradicated
Nor are they divorced from the function of the mind
Those who in engage in fierce debate
Are passionate about the beliefs they define

There are easy competing mistakes to make
Truth and desire are in conflict, yet congruent
When they are broken apart the soul aches
Soon the mind and heart wander discontent

Constant tension exists between the two
Desires can deceive . . . but so too can the mind
Wisdom we must all accrue
To ensure we do not become eternally blind

Many seek the solitary route
Believing truth can be found unaided
But such a road will not bear fruit
For knowledge is always interrelated

There is no easy way to parse truth from lies
Destined to fail, all should still try
For truth is worth endless attempts
Preventing desires the mind to preempt

The muscles of the mind and heart
Require continuous, careful thought
Making it easy to observe
Why mindless societies are perverse

When all desires are affirmed as good
No mental effort need be exerted
Truth is set aside for eternal childhood
Ruled by desires, reality is inverted

The Past

Of all areas of dispute, the past reigns supreme
In hindsight much of reality becomes easy to observe
Still other aspects of what occurred are hard to fathom
The events themselves over time become obscured
From the present point of view, the past creates a wide chasm

Understanding one another and the society we inhabit
Is impossible without a functional knowledge of our past
How can we rise to this impossible task
The uncertainty leaves humanity downcast

Studying events long ended teaches many lessons
From the fragments of human deception emerges a reliable story
For truth arises from the ashes of even the worst oppression

The need to study history is not a provocative claim
But different versions of events war in this domain
There are few "consensus facts" for interpretations vary
Desires within men battle, leading us to weep and worry

Why study a discipline wrought with infinite error?
How can we resolve the competing narratives?

In truth history cannot be divorced
From other forms of knowledge
Beliefs one brings may reinforce
Observation of past sources

This is no justification for needless suspicion
Philosophic assumptions are age-old foundations
Worldviews stand before our eyes like a prism
Givens are necessary in the mental chain of causation

What makes us fear this simple truth
Every era makes many mistakes
Modern lies our minds do soothe
Causing considerable heartache

The world never moved towards linear progress
Epochs trade various intellectual deficiencies
No new ideas will pull us out of distress
For humanity lacks self-sufficiency

The past will remain in dispute
Wise men know history rhymes
Lies will remain for good to refute
Until the end of time

THE ILLUSION OF SELF

Look in the mirror, what do you see?
You may say, my eyes land on "me"
But who are you, how can a person be defined
When the entirety of their being is divided and misaligned?

What you call "self" is an abstract fiction
Communal—yet separate—individuals must wrestle
With internal doubt and deep affliction
Am I myself or merely a social vessel?

Tension between rights and responsibilities
Gives all a moment of pause
There exists a clear impracticability
In attempting to reconcile freedom and law

Despite this paradox, both are imperative
The wise set sail to understand why
While the fool either curses law as pejorative
Or creates senseless rules in an effort to simplify

Both efforts are equally futile and flawed
Relying on opposite, yet complementary facades
Those devoted to these human deceptions
Create knowledge to support their misconceptions

And thus youth study distorted knowledge
First to prepare, then to complete college
After years of study they are not an inch nearer
To understanding who they observe in the mirror

THE ILLUSION OF RELATIONSHIP

Conversation, eye contact, light touch
We call these signs of human connection
It is tempting to read far too much
Into outward indications of affection

What lies behind the mind and heart of another
Remains outside each man's grasp
Even the love of your own mother
May be nothing more than a necessary mask

Love, devotion, loyalty and admiration
Are not outwardly identifiable
Seeking surety we observe causation
Saying love is externally verifiable

From this flawed foundation
Pain is unavoidable . . . always inevitable
Leaving us ready to interpret each sensation
As a sign that love is real and credible

Then when heartache comes to call
We wonder why we loved at all

Two natural, normal common responses
Reveal the depths of human delusion
Cynics hide behind pain, eschewing nuance
Yet the romantic argues away relational illusion

From birth all are biologically hardwired
To seek deep, meaningful communal ties
But within the limits of the human condition
We cannot know if our lives rest on lies

The motivations behind "loving" actions
Matter more than we can know
When all relations are reduced to transactions
We sully the soil in which beauty grows

Love becomes cheap, diminished to a commodity
Instead of seeking depth in one another
We pretend as if humanity is mere property
Searching for quick pleasure, our souls we smother

Still, today as in all eras, human souls need divine mediation
To break the bridge dividing our souls . . . a passage to relational
  reconciliation
A way to pierce the illusion and make us whole
A way to break from evolving, yet forced social roles

THE ILLUSION OF CONTROL

Create your own happiness
And you will surely find peace
You can mold this worldly mess
To create what your soul seeks

Control is at your fingertips
Do not play the victim!
Victimhood is a sinking ship
That destroys many men

Control the world around you
Find a way to create
Conditions that allow you to subdue
Pain and negative fate

As you grapple with control
Make sure to always ignore
The eternal state of your soul
This avenue you must not explore

Instead control your surroundings
To avoid the searing pain
That comes with the internal sound
Of a reality that would drive you insane

Truth is what you create!
Your mind must never forget
You control whether you feel the weight
Of deep, existential threat

Control itself is an illusion
Happiness cannot be created
It is hard to come to this conclusion
We like dominion over our inner state

In truth control can only be narrowly asserted
Nature and nurture are intertwined
Deeply influencing the adult person
Directly, we control merely the contents of our mind

SILENT SUFFERING

To suffer alone is to walk as an alien
In a world where your pain is viewed as distant
Agony, discomfort, sorrow all felt in vain
When expressed others react with resistance

The neat categories developed by modern philosophies
Fail to account for the complexity of reality
Condensed to five senses, human pain is stifled
And the deepest wounds are viewed as small and trifle

For pain and harm cannot be defined sans context
Without understanding goodness pain loses its meaning
In this fragmented world we wonder perplexed
Unaware of how our minds are trained to refuse redeeming

Suffering is seen as nothing more than material
Money and riches will surely solve the problem!
So we move to become more entrepreneurial
Only to find ourselves closer to rock bottom

Some swing from one pendulum to another

Wealth is finite, we must redistribute monetary resources
Yet no amount of reallocation reduces the pain
For there is no swift or easy societal recourse
Leading to a place where contentment can be sustained

Why do we seek universal solutions to the problem of pain?
What makes us assume man can banish suffering
Through the rearranging of social hierarchies and plans?
The wise man sees such as a solution as puzzling

But there is a logic to this folly
It keeps us perpetually externally fixated
And we would rather not face the melancholy
For pain will never be fully eradicated

A constant battle with material poverty
Keeps minds preoccupied and distracted
Erecting a barrier to thoughtful curiosity
That wisely teaches pain is also abstracted

Observe your pain and seek to give it a name
Do you notice a resistance, do those around you refuse
Perhaps their philosophy is why they lace you with shame
For those who cannot define harm fail to see abuse

Investigate the dungeon of your own mind
Who do you torture, mock, and treat as swine?
Do not lie to yourself, look at your soul's state
Does your suffering breed empathy or hate?

PROJECTED PAIN

Unaddressed pain is a dangerous weapon
It has created incalculable victims
The hurt heart is easily threatened
Overreacting to protect her wounded system

Undefined agony breeds evil pathologies
For without the ability to access care
The deeply wounded seek a philosophy
To take them out of their unbearable snare

When pain cannot be expressed it does not evaporate
Instead, its roots dig deeper self-watered by internal tears
Daunted by the intensity, society fears to enter the gates
Instead choosing to squash the aching heart for years

This buried discomfort confronts us periodically
Modern woman is a master at misidentifying what she sees
Instead of questioning, she reacts illogically
Eager to find offense in the expression she perceives

Instead of examining what society views as harmful
The blind would lead us to believe
Pain unknown to experts must be viewed with scorn
Those hated by social power find no relief

Men who view the therapist with skepticism
Are routinely mocked for their masculinity
They must not deride the modern prophets with cynicism
For these definitions flow from professional divinity

As technological capacity grows
The ability to stifle unwanted pain expands
Social authorities bake their assumptions into code
Making it easy to identify the undesirables to ban

Thus, pain continues to project outward
Perverted authority runs from its reflection
While those who face suffering stumble and flounder
Agony compounds, society is engulfed in a sea of depression

With the human condition categorized as a disease
People transform into experiential projects
Instead of seeking to heal through the process of grief
Minds and bodies are infected with the pain of neglect

THE SEVEN DEADLY SINS

Conflicting voices reside inside
Allegiance to good is transitory
What should serve as our guide?
What spirit leads the human story?

Is good difficult to cultivate?
Does each person wrestle with sin?
Or is the idea of evil designed to suffocate
By crushing the confidence of men?

If evil were fictitious why does pain sting?
When suffering the soul cries for relief
It is impossible to justify all things
Attempting such a feat bastardizes grief

Understanding suffering requires a concept of sin
Those beneath the weight of sorrow know this well
Thus the wise set aside temporal pleasure and begin
To learn the internal vices that manifest hell

Pride

Pride often hides behind self-respect
Pretending to provide the soul rest
But pride the heart does not protect
Instead it puts each man to the test

Pride convinces the mind to hide
By telling man he is always right
Pride trains our hearts to reject strife
Why struggle when you are always right?

Insidiously pride closes the mind
Shutting man off from the gift of learning
The prideful wander lost and blind
Fearful of the good for which they are yearning

There is a kernel of truth dwelling in pride's deceit
Self-hatred is surely not a virtue
Those whose lives have been degraded and beaten
Are right to assert their infinite value

Still self-respect is not synonymous with pride
Understanding humanity's innate worth is wise
Pride exceeds health leaving the soul bound and tied
Rendering man incapable of compromise

Once pride takes root the soul begins to rot
Enchanted by pride's moral justification
Man believes what he deems good should be sought
For others' beliefs he makes no accommodation

Lust

Lust is associated with sexual desires
Allowing many lustful men to hide
Lust affects numerous internal trials
Requiring excess to become satisfied

Some pervert virtue by glorifying lust
Categorizing excess desire as good
Thus destroying the basis of sound trust
In the service of praising falsehood

Desires themselves should be acknowledged
For burying fact only destroys truth
Still to all desires we should not pay homage
Such a disposition only leads to abuse

Lust distorts healthy human aspirations
Wealth, sex, and pleasure are beautiful gifts
Excess in practice erodes joy's foundation
Leaving the world's powerful successful yet adrift

Gluttony

The word gluttony is associated with food
An unfortunate reduction of the term
Gluttony refers to a compulsive attitude
One that every consumptive desire affirms

The gluttonous heart is insatiable
Desires and actions have a broken relation
Of moderation this soul is incapable
Gluttony serves as an internal dictator

Colloquially gluttony is now called addiction
Like many sins it is treated as a mental illness
Many live in a harmful, senseless fiction
Convinced they cannot solve what plagues their senses

Gluttony and addiction can be solved through action
Men and women exist not in a helpless condition
All can change their internal disposition
Each can bring desires under their submission

Greed

Greed is universally condemned and practiced
Those who decry its evils embody this vice
We look down on those with less wealth or social status
As if earthly success were the pinnacle of life

Greed is more than seeking material pleasure
It places cheap blessings before lasting peace
Greed makes worldly standards its measure
Fearful of watching significance decrease

Greed destroys the best of human relationship
Reducing people to their hierarchical standing
The capacity to seek just character is stripped
The greedy to shallow qualities cling

As with other vices greed is sly
Striving to meet human needs is not a fault
Thoughtlessly, many reason defy
Unable to know when they have what was sought

Greed has no ceiling; more is never enough
Wisdom knows when to set sufficient limits
For the mindless consumption of material stuff
Devalues the beauty of the human spirit

Envy

Unchecked greed moves into envy
A perverse focus on the success of others
The envious may appear friendly
But the smile serves only as a dark cover

"He has more while working fewer hours"
"She does not deserve an easy life"
Over others the envious seek to gain power
Eager to reallocate humanity's strife

Arrogantly, the envious believe their own fiction
Convinced they can best distribute finite resources
Surely, they can alleviate human affliction
Through the use of authority and control

When envy governs social relations
People grow suspicious of one another
In the air is an unspoken expectation
One man's gain causes another to suffer

Thus, envy destroys the soul's essence
Tearing down the predicates of brotherly love
When envy rules love is not present
Instead wills battle one another to rise above

Sloth

In a world where comfort is idolized
And new rights are invented overnight
A life of hard work is scandalized
Viewed as the worst of human plights

Working for a lifetime and earning little
Is seen as a punishment to mortal man
Without external glory many are brittle
The modern mind is nothing if not vain

Slothfulness often harbors hidden nihilism
The risk of working without reward is rejection
Effort without success is perceived as a prison
No different from Sisyphus's perpetual dejection

The sloth is more than merely lazy
He suffers not from procrastination
Work itself he sees as unnecessary
Unless it creates his ideal situation

Thus, slothfulness stands not on its own
It accompanies other forms of depravity
Nurturing iniquity causes evil to grow
Making goodness more difficult to perceive

Wrath

Anger is the easiest vice to condemn
Observing rage makes most uncomfortable
Still, some embrace the act of revenge
Regardless of damage done to the vulnerable

Resentment drives actions of the vengeful
Unfair suffering lives beneath this snare
The unwise and impulsive are uncareful
Caught in the abyss of anguish and despair

Rather than processing pain, anger is nurtured
Until the mind is convinced violence is justice
Aggression is necessary fairness to further
Says the man whose sorrow has crushed him

The wrath of man is not like the divine
It does not accurately distinguish right from wrong
Man's violence compounds suffering and decline
It causes the weak to die and feeds pride to the strong

This wrath incentivizes man to glorify power
Vulnerability is seen as the worst condition
When wrath rises beauty is cowered
And the world becomes a brutal competition

Wrath hides behind righteous indignation
Is violence not the voice of the unheard?
Yet wielding anger justly is its rarest application
Swiftly shedding blood is what the fool prefers

Revenge is the wine of the unwise
Drunk on vice he pursues his plan
Violence gives society more to despise
Unnecessarily extending suffering's lifespan

OPPRESSION

COST & CONSEQUENCE

Cause and effect
Cost and consequence
Instinctively we protect
Our mind from providence

Instead, we seek meaning
In shallow material spaces
Turning reality into a dream
Goodness we quickly debase

Why does he have more than I?
When I toil all day and he barely tries?

Insidiously envy enters our mind
Soon polluting our hearts
Putting out our eyes, we become blind

VICTIM OF CIRCUMSTANCE

Why must I bear this burden?
This question is often queried
For life is painful and absurd
Difficulties leave us helpless and weary

Some have endless earthly wealth
While other lives in squalor
This reality harms a comrade's mental health
Inequality he seeks to make smaller

"I shall rob Peter to pay Paul
No one deserves boundless prosperity
Over wealth and land man should not brawl
Let us force the rich to give to charity!"

Across the globe schemes to bring equality
Have resulted in mass death and carnage
Compassion at gunpoint poisons the polity
While inequality rages on unassuaged

Communism kills, just ask its victims
Those whose voices cry from the grave
Their lives were destroyed, and reality turned grim
Due to the efforts of those who claimed to save
Earth from evil, imperialist days

Despite the millions who died at the hands of social change
Intelligentsia idolizes those who sought false equality
A communal future will not turn out the same!
Say those who believe they can perfectly impose morality

"If only we abandon the desire for profit
Then surely we may all live in peace"
The naïve believe this nonsensical promise
Unable to fathom the harshness of reality

For victims of circumstances will always remain
Despite communism's endless refrain
Capitalism does not create evil
But death always accompanies social upheaval

Look to the east at what the communist hides
Millions whose bodies lie still without life
This is the legacy the Marxist refuses to look in the eye
For it proves their idealism requires bloodletting and strife

Instead, they gloss over the sins of their heroes
Crying out for the destruction of all victims
Their minds remain constricted and narrow
Unable to fathom the death created by their system

THE PROGRESSIVE MAN

Deceptive, hubristic, narrow-minded
Blindly trusting, how perverse!
Ears and eyes closed to justice
Truth he seeks to subvert

Rudderless and vapid
His mind turns to mush
Instinctively he lashes out
All dissenting views to crush

Purity of mind is his heaven
Only the holy pass to this place
But as the canon evolves
Incessant fears he cannot shake!

This fear destroys discernment
Spiraling, downward he falls
Into the depths of despair
Bound by ever harsher laws

PROGRESSIVE OPPRESSION

Holy, heaven, nature, sin
These are now merely trends

The canon has been opened
Revelation is accepted
Shh . . . be careful what you say
Soon, it may get you arrested

Despite what we say
Our doctrines are fixed
Culture we seek to fray
By playing mental tricks

Manipulation and deceit
Are the weapons of choice
We are not afraid to cheat
Rules should not constrain *God's* voice

We seek to shape society to our holy vision
Welcome to a world ruled by progressive religion

Doctrine of God

God is dead, have you not heard?!
He died last century
Stop reading His word
And set your mind at ease!

A new regime has arisen
It is popular and plain
Do whatever you desire
For we have banished shame!

That is absurd, shame still exists
It is part of being human, and will always persist

Besides, shame is not innately negative
It can act as a beacon
Leading us to be contemplative
And better understand reason

Oh, and who are you to lay down rules?
Did you not just announce
That all could do as they choose
This predicate . . . do you denounce?

Stop! No more questions
You're right . . . there *are* exceptions

The rule to do as you please was never absolute
There is one whose will you *must* salute

This is unfair and fraudulent
An absolute is God, by *definition*

No, God is loving, absolutes are not
And we slayed the divine
Now we are left with raw power
And power is *never* benign

With God dead, there is only force and compulsion
And if you object . . . you'll guarantee your own expulsion

Doctrine of Sin

Sin used to mean a transgression
Of a perfect criteria
But now it means an expression
Against society's "morally superior"

Speech . . . we must regulate!
Scream young generations
For hearing something they hate
May cause internal consternation

It could even lead to *independent thought*
The gravest of social sins
And no one wants to be caught
Eating with one of *them*

Society is about community
And endless affirmation
Questions bring disunity
Intimidating this hive religion

Free thought is sin . . . you *must* approve
Beliefs held by the majority
If after warnings you refuse
We will invoke forceful authority

Secular Hell

Hell is separation from God
Enlightened man has—of course—abandoned
This wild, conspiratorial fraud
And replaced it with another idea to defend

Without God, only man remains
Thus, community is supreme
Banishment takes on new shame
You must follow the mainstream

If life on earth is all that exists
Why risk communal abandonment?
Hand us your mind, do not resist
And we will let you live in content

But if you refuse to bow before
Laws crafted by elite prowess
You will be ridiculed as deplorable
Abandoned to solitary madness

Which religion is more cruel?

One gives man a lifetime to choose
He either believes or play the eternal fool

The other offers a false choice
Accept our law or never have a voice

Hell has not been subdued
Don't let seculars fool you
The idea lives in their ideology
It has simply been reframed
To keep your mind in their chains

Fearing social dissociation
People crouch and cower
Perpetually afraid
The mob will come for them one hour

Progressive Prophet

Solemnly they approach their pulpit
Intent on imparting doctrinal wisdom
To the poor, lost souls who sit
Under the weight of youthful indecision

The ritual begins as the bell rings
He opens his remarks, I am here to help you see
Truth does not exist, it is all subjective
But thankfully it has revealed itself to me!

If you listen to my voice and obey my words
In this course you will learn and . . . receive an A
Just follow along with the herd
Never question what *I* say

Professor, on what authority do you presume to act?
Who made you god of the rules governing society?
You petulant fool, my superior intellect
Gives me the right to rule over thee

It is hard work updating the evolving cannon
I have no time for your skepticism
I must work to slay the dragon
Of evil imperial capitalism!

Now . . . quiet, the rules governing society
Must be updated by someone who understands morality
The people await my edicts, and with every passing hour
Journalists panic, unsure of what to tell their audience to devour!

My child, your morals are already out of date
I must not make the public wait!
My revelation is of utmost necessity
For I am part of earth's secular deity

Progressive Preacher

Preachers learn theology from religious scholars
They perform well in school and devour knowledge
After their release from scholastic pursuits
They are eager to share their truth

Impatient to tear down social constructs
Convinced they cannot err
For they learned to deconstruct
From Rousseau, Derrida, and professor Kerr

They represent the marginalized
Those harmed by oppressive religions
But these enlightened women have canonized
Love, unity, and a collective vision

Now a Love Wins sticker is on the breast
Of a heated, angry activist
"Fuck you whore, I hope you die!"
'Tis love that made her yell this cry

For to usher in a new and better reality
War must be waged on ignorance
So that good people may live in harmony
Without questions or other belligerence

"They hate us and want us to go extinct!"
Say those who have been trained to think
There is only one acceptable position
For no one can dissent from the *holy mission*

Progressive Pupil

Train them when they're young, my professor said
Then you can control them until they're dead
Pupils are not people in progressive eyes
Merely soldiers who can be trained to rise

Against the traditions of the West
A civilization the left detests

Its art and heroes are passe
A modern mind cannot understand
What our founders had to say

They wrote documents defining equality
Works oft cited as the epitome of morality
Yet from these men they cannot learn
Instead, tradition they smugly spurn

"They were immoral, full of malice
Corrupted by ideas of the past
We modern men are no longer callous
Our fathers sins leave us aghast!"

Yet listen to their words and hear
Quotes from those whom they mock and jeer

Do they know of whom they plagiarize
Or are they unable to analyze
The flaws within their own beliefs
Ah! I forget in logic they do not believe!

For the "good" student only sees through the lens of learned
    identity

And thus, the "tolerant" are taught to strip humanity of its dignity

WHAT IS CRIME?

Crime is a transgression of the law
Violations lead to loss of freedom
But who chooses what is barred?
What authority places you in prison?

Law and morality cannot be separated
For law supports justice
All actions cannot be tolerated
Inclusion is a lie, it cannot be practiced

Questioning the basis of legal canon
Can be a dangerous game
The temptation to justify passion
Causes some to lose the refining effects of shame

But not to question is equally intolerable
For unjust legal regimes are dishonorable

To distinguish between just and corrupt
A fundamental analysis must be conducted
Yet, it is the height of ignorance to disrupt
A sound legal system deserving your trust

And so, we are left with a difficult truth
Wisdom demands we abandon our ignorant youth
Without a sound basis for universal morality
Social order should not bow before new orthodoxy

THE SHADOW OF DEATH

Societal norms inform
Perceptions of morality
Questions bring trouble & scorn . . .
We hate to see our brutality

Terms of moral discussion
Begin with a priori thought
First premise moves to conclusion
Until we find what we have sought

But, alas! What do we find?
Is it truth we now behold?
Or did reason make us blind?
Did the mind construct a mold?

The whole of truth is elusive
It is not easy to determine
What defines the word abusive?
The answer alters with time

Eras come and morals change
Yet harm is always ignored
The silent tremble in shame
Unable to give pain words

Identifying the abused
Is always an easy task
Whose pain do we refuse?
Who is forced to wear a mask?

Men are toxic, therapists say
Full of violent impulses
Women never on others prey
Females for righteousness revolt

Thus, with societal license
Women are free to abuse
For no mental contrivance
Can pierce feminism's excuse

Women determine life's worth
Women alone possess this right
She confers value before birth
Or with violence life she smites

Is this aggression justified?
Must equality rest on gore?
Let us explore the silent cries
From a human feminists abhor

Unwanted children fear to speak the truth
Why invite the anger of feminine brutes?
Still, silent stories must escape the lips
Despite forming the ugliest of scripts

*Act one begins when human breath is stifled
by the shadow of death*

In the privacy of the American home
Children face the tragedy of equality
"If only I had foresight *before* you were born!
Now killing you is not a possibility!"

Internally, the child wonders—what of my birth?
Why is my presence a painful, cosmic mistake
"If I am good enough, I can prove my worth
Then from this nightmare I will surely awake"

"Horrid child you are disobedient and cruel
Do you not know I sacrificed my freedom for *you*
I birthed you, and *I* gave you life, you are *my* jewel
Yet you give me no honor . . . your maker you abuse!

"No! You are harsh and hateful. No one owns my soul
You are a monster, consumed by evil desires!"
These words brought mother into sarcastic control
"Child, *I* alone preserved you from death by pliers

You have no rights aside from that which I assign
Ask any legal scholar or modern ethicist
Your pathetic, petulant, irrational whines
Mean nothing in a world ruled by female instinct"

Cowering in fear, the child would cry—but why?
What good would tears bring, it lifts not the tyranny
Defeated and dejected, child turned a blind eye
"She spoke no lies, my worth has no guarantee"

Days turn to years, there is no relief from this hell
Each mistake brings torment and endless derision
There was no comfort, no listening ear to tell
Those who hear will think mother made the wrong decision

"Abortion is mercy," child had heard the phrase before
Would I be better off dead? she must ask herself
Is it not better to die than to live abhorred?
Into darkness and despair her soul did melt

This is only act one in the story of hate
Granting the legal right to kill comes at a cost
When death is a right pain does not ever abate
Those harmed by the law wander alone and lost

"If I had the foresight to exercise my rights
I would have been spared my child's ugly sight!"

"Why must mother hate me, do I not deserve breath?"
Asks the child who lives under the shadow of death

Act two comes when pain arrives and professionals care deprive

Death's shadow followed the child like a bad dream
Destruction lingered forever on her mind
A series of cruel games this was her life's theme
Her desires were perverse; she hated all mankind!

For internal peace, she sought professional care
Walking into the office she sensed her own fear
Why did it feel as if death lingered in the air?
She shrugged it off, help surely resided in here

Pen in hand . . . therapy session swiftly began
"What is the problem giving rise to your deep pain?"
Ignoring the sinister eyes of the woman
"My name is half-aborted, this drives me insane"

"Surely the patriarchy is prevailing!
Your father's sins caused your mother's lack of love
If your mother had left religious failings
She would have treated you as a gift from above!"

"Do not lie to me—look me in the eye and speak truth
Do you believe she had the right to kill my life?"
"My child there is no truth, you speak as a youth
But, you must accept abortion is a *woman's right*

This right gives you options and an equal voice
Do not act out of irrational, blinding pain
Your mother made infinitely wise choices
The patriarchy is keeping your heart in chains!"

From the room the child fled, searching for health
Soon on another couch she sat in fearful hope
This therapist was a liar, but moved in stealth
Retelling the child mindless social tropes

"Abortion is both a right and a trauma
Denying women autonomy is a bad rule
Never speak ill of the motives of your mama
She did her best, even if to you it *felt* cruel"

The child fled again . . . to another office
No matter where she went the result was the same
Until, overcome by the pain, she grew incautious
Each day brought agony, she moved to end her shame

Pills she swallowed, alcohol she freely consumed
Suicide she tried, but her attempt failed
All was dark, dreary, full of endless gloom
To death and destruction she was forever nailed

There is no access to care for children like her
Still, one last time, she tried secular support
The psychiatrist's first words were modern slurs
"Mothers love their girls and have the right to abort"

Dejected, the child hung her head in anger
"Does no one see the blatant hypocrisy?
How can they mindlessly to my heart pander
While defending a tyrannical matriarchy?"

*Act three shows hope never dies for goodness
always crushes lies*

There was only one who rejected this narrative
He was kind and the child he supported
"Child, do not listen!" was his declarative
You have inherent worth, there is no just abortion

"Your mother is a liar and a cruel brute
Her intentions were for evil, do not be fooled
Those who dismiss you feel pain that is acute
The agony you face makes them appear cruel

No one on earth has the right to define your worth
This is equally true of both men and women
You have the inherent right to a life and birth
Women, like men, seek to justify their worst sins

Do not accept death as a price you must pay
Do not take on your mother's despicable shame
Fight for your life and evil you will slay
Look at reality and correctly assign blame

The world you inhabit is infinitely flawed
Do not let broken femininity your soul steal
Transcend vice, do not be lured by false gods
Fall not into the resentment you now feel"

From his wisdom she perpetually drank
His love, peace, and grace, gave her rest
He held her at bay, into death she never sank
Until, over time, she considered herself blessed

He held no license, nor any formal degree
But beauty and goodness he helped her to see
And instead of living in infinite strife
She embraced a full, regenerated life

There remains hope for the endlessly oppressed
Those whose hearts are crushed by secular religion
The victims hide among society's depressed
Fearful of naming their irreverent condition

Now you have walked through the shadow of secular death
How much longer must we leave these souls alone in stress
How much longer will the inclusive leave unaddressed
The plight of the hated progressives freely oppress?

COMPASSION OR CRUELTY?

For decades the womb transformed into a tomb
Until one June day death itself was slain
This brings history to a new chapter
What follows is a story that matters

Justification for violence is nothing new
First, it was men who perfected deadly systems
Then, seeking equality women thought to use
Bloodshed as a way to equalize gender conditions

For a chapter of our history
This right was granted by decree

The value and worth of humanity
Were viewed as subjective rather than innate
Allowing unerring femininity
Individual worth to freely adjudicate

One woman held sole dominion
Over the life of her offspring
A person's value was subject to her opinion
At her bidding, children tasted death's sting

Women chose souls to desecrate
Compassion was invoked, "it is mercy!" they contended
Having learned from men, many justified targeted hate
And celebrated death as a precious right to defend

Death's Destruction

The legal ruling announced one year
Forever changed the social landscape
It drew a line crystal and clear
From this reality there is no escape

Many have argued the ruling unfair
"It is a human rights violation!
Women can kill what is rightfully theirs
It is wrong to force them through gestation"

After the Court made its decision
Many abortion clinics were forced to close
And now it is known with precision
Specific births are because of what the Court chose

These children are in their infant years
When they grow older they will surely see
Whether they are viewed as precious and dear
Or the result of an evil decree

For the danger of hate is oft discussed
As a blight on civil society
Animosity leads to disgust
From destruction the wise always flee

But hatred forever hides in plain sight
Each generation claims compassion
Until the despised bring into light
Scars caused by trendy moral canons

Those serious about empathy
Analyze culture to predict
The rising young facing enmity
To ignore their pain is derelict

Past abuses are easy to perceive
Hindsight will always be 20/20
Of current abuse we are deceived
What is defended will be judged only by history

Death Glorified

It is now the year twenty thirty-eight
The year a child grappled with her fate

Lisa grew up just one square mile
From the now abandoned clinic
School taught her the decision was vile
To fit in, social morals she mimicked

If her mother's human rights were denied
Her life is a consequence of oppression
When the clinic closed her mother cried
For mom birth was an act of aggression

From the world Lisa learned to hide
She pretends to be loved and wanted
"Abortion is merciful" her friends cry
Despite the façade her soul is haunted

Suffering should be extinguished
No one should live a life of abuse
Women who abort kindly relinquish
The life of a person with no value

These phrases she continually hears
If not for pride she would be reduced to tears

The Cost of Dehumanization

Social messages confuse Lisa's mind
How can death ever be considered kind?
In dark conflict she finds herself entwined
If she speaks her pain she will be maligned

All professions affirm the right to abort
She had never seen the matter debated
Except in the oppressive Supreme Court
"My comrades are right" she said, yet felt degraded

One day she rode past the clinic with friends
"Have you thought of those born after Dobbs?
I pity them, their lives should have ended"
Lisa heard these words and held back sobs

When she returned home she spoke to herself
For out loud she could not utter these words
Into her mind the agony did melt
And this is what Lisa alone heard.

Doubting Dehumanization

"Why is abortion a human right?
Why am I not allowed to question
My life I must hide as a thief in night
While inside I fight with depression

School books tell me to always be kind
Offensive words I must never express
Are those around me senseless and blind
Is it not clear their words can cause distress?

The world is full of hypocrites and fools
I should not view my birth as a mistake
There are places where birth is seen as good
Once eighteen I will move to such a state"

Defiance sat beside endless guilt
"If only I were braver than I am
Exposing myself will get me killed
Social death is the weapon of women

Like others I take the easy way out
Afraid to speak what is plainly true
I live in perpetual doubt
Afraid others will learn I am abused

Society loathes people like me
I am a useless minority
Not part of progressive priorities
They tell me of my inferiority

Would they speak this way if they knew?
Or would they hold their thoughts inside
Why does it matter what words they spew?
Either way they will wish I had died"

Communal Choice: Compassion or Cruelty?

Lisa's story has only now commenced
She cannot yet read loathsome headlines
Will she be forced to play mental defense?
Will she be treated as worse than swine?
Will the "tolerant" care about her life?

Or will she be treated as a mistake
Someone's whose life should never have been
Will she hear from those who claim to be awake
She was birthed from an original sin?

Now this story is hypothetical
Our culture could change its ugly ways
Alas, this change would be heretical
Self-reflection society has slain

Deconstruction is only for religion
And abortion is a secular dogma
It stands above moral criticism
Progressives do not question their mamas

Some children are doomed to social demise
The empathetic look on them with respect
Telling them death should be despised
Even when others their worth reject

The twin lies of inclusion and compassion
Are now more than ever clear and concise
Moral superiority of mothers is the mission
Thus, killing is coded as a form of kindness

The "woke" sit atop their ivory towers
Ostracizing worthless minorities
Unwanted children do not increase power
For women vote in much higher quantities

One day there will be an examination
Rejecting this marginalization
And the subjugated will expose brutality
For what it is, not compassion, but cruelty

How you treat these children is up to you
From this day forward don't say you never knew

HOPE

FEARFUL TO CHANGE

"You are perfect the way you are!"

What a horrible lie!
It keeps many cage-bound
Unable to strive

Or create a meaningful map

For life cannot be traversed
Without a compass to guide
And that compass is broken
If you pretend you are fine

You are not perfect
You could be much more
Ignore the voices
Who tell you not to explore

The depth of your depravity
For evil within you runs deep
Reflect on your duality
You cannot fix what you refuse to see

Don't appease the masses
Never agree with what you believe to be untrue
The world is not improved by lies
Even those we believe to be polite

Speak kindly to all, but disagree
For truth cannot be known
If you live to appease

Those fearful to change hate your dissent
But speak your mind, never relent
For popular opinion is nearly always wrong
And cannot be improved if you stifle your song

THE POWER OF WORDS

Words can kill or save
Heal or cut deep
Place, pierce, or misbehave
With what spirit should we speak?

Control of words
Must not be central
Reducing men to herds
Unable to see the transcendental

Freedom that speech brings
The liberty to think as one pleases
Free to talk and to sing
With no regard who one appeases

The morality of our age
Rigid, unyielding, unwilling to change
Modern orthodoxy is a cage
Fearful of the free exchange

Of unfettered human thought
Which unseats many a king
For truth diligently sought
Withstands arrows the liars sling

FREEWILL

If nature and nurture determine our identity
Do we own what is our humanity?

Why not seek to control the lives of children
What makes it cruel to indoctrinate?
Is it not better to kill the small villains
By seeking small minds to dominate?

In principle education no longer seeks
To generate logically sound thought
Instead it produces mild and meek
People who believe whatever they are taught

In an attempt to build manmade utopia
Educators work to destroy the mind
Teaching the opium of endless phobias
Incentivizing children to become mentally blind

Unable to think for themselves
Endlessly dependent
Inside their minds fear dwells
School destroys their independence

The mental colonizers cheer
Happy to see the fruit of their labors
Free will they wish to disappear
For free thinkers do not need human saviors

And manmade morality is what they wish to impose
On every population inhabiting earth
Thus religious factions are their foes
Because they teach people to observe

The standards that transcend man's mind
Pointing people to the love of the divine
A love man cannot perfectly replicate
Therefore calling us the divine to investigate

This could lead to the demolition
Of flawed social planners
Whose artificial wisdom
Retains power through control and slander

Let society accept a simple predicate
All individuals must be free
To determine which values they accept
Rather than accepting popular secular creeds

DISSECTING DESIRE

Longing for an object or outcome
Is a natural human disposition
But where do these desires come from?
What is done when cravings face competition?

Yearning fits within the system of life
All wants cannot be fulfilled
Choosing between desires is a cause of strife

Journey through desires
To understand yourself
Five truths you will acquire
Adding to wisdom's wealth

The first truth is simple to explain
Not all desires can be entertained

Desire & Time

Choices are exercised at a specific time
But their consequences reverberate
Once an action occurs it cannot be declined
With the past you cannot debate

Longings change like the weather
Choices rooted in instinct
Are flighty as a feather

Decisions made without contemplation
Are subjected to endless rumination
For acting without adequate thought
Leads a man to become distraught

This leads to a second straightforward truth
Processes drive the decisions you choose

Decisions Are Procedural

Still, even he who is ready to think
Struggles his desires to understand
Either from desires he is taught to shrink
Or to embrace each whim as a command

Integrating desires into personhood
Comprehending the proper role of feelings
Would break the bonds of modern brotherhood
Modern man has no patience in relational dealings

In a world where all longings are by definition good
An invisible prison is erected between humanity
Each person is daily different, yet perpetually misunderstood
Constructing a cohesive identity is deemed insanity

Thought processes become rushed and scrambled
This is a central feature of the secular mind
If all human desires are equally worthy examples
Those who ponder the goodness of their choices are unwise

Modern thought's perpetual confusion reveals reality
Defining all desires as a good is a fashionable fallacy

Desires Are Deceptive

All desires are equal, but some are more equal than others
The message behind the madness reveals
How modern morality our minds does smother
Pointing the human spirit to an unspoken ideal

For the limits of time forever demand
Some yearnings be celebrated
While others fiercely condemned

Knowing desires is a complicated pursuit
Belief and desire operate within the same system
Do beliefs or desires reside at the root
To understand yourself requires deep wisdom

Working with the tools of modern thought
Deep wisdom is unlikely to be sought
Instead the mind will rot and atrophy
Seeking only temporal bodily ecstasy

The fourth truth exposes the risk of impulsive action
Poor decisions lead to a lifetime of dissatisfaction

Decisions Compound

Ill thought-out decisions are akin
To a boulder rolling down a steep hill
When the first action initially begins
The rock threatens no one to kill

But each desire acted quickens the pace
Accepting past mistakes is an unbearable cost
Just as a boulder crushes those in its wake
The man consumed by passion is forever lost

The last truth is difficult to hear, but impossible to change
Desires will always conflict, they never remain the same

Desires Diverge

The antidote to poor decision-making
Rejects the foundation of modern advice
Drink this medicine by not partaking
In the belief all feelings are right

Abandon the impulse to act sans contemplation
Adopt the mindset of the present-day rebel
Those who take this path prefer isolation
For vacuous pleasure they cannot settle

Confusion natural to human experience
Reveals solitude's appropriate mission
Rather than making errors ever more serious
Wisdom is the fulfillment of internal discussion

LOVE & LIBERTY

Is liberty boundless lack of restraint?
Are rules harmful and archaic?
Or are boundaries the portal allowing us to paint
A human depiction of a grand mosaic

Rules alone provide necessary conditions
For the soul to open and bloom
Without rules nothing is certain
And the mind must to threats be attuned

In a state of perpetual uncertainty
Aspects of your soul cannot be free
Instead waking hours are spent
Working to avoid suffering and lament

Yet rules are risky and dangerous
Impose the wrong ones and harm will come
Stripping men and women of their purpose
Liberty and love should act as one

Internally we all wrestle with this predicament
None of us are assured of the right balance
Between tyranny and rules fostering contentment
This is evidenced through our confused parlance

The murky difficulty in seeking to live free
Is stifled by reductionist cliches
Leaving humanity unable to see
The rules of love keep evil at bay

TRIBUTE TO BONHOEFFER: THE COST OF DISCIPLESHIP

Cheap Grace

The gift that keeps on giving
Boundless and free
It justifies continued sinning
For its blessings flow for all eternity

Grace with no corresponding cost
Is easy to acquire
Tempting us our souls to toss
Turning the divine into satire

Extending grace is enticing
It is viewed as compassionate
And so we go on advising
The affirmation all actions as adequate

After all the boundless foundation of grace
Will every sin surely erase
Judgment is scorned; shame is reprimanded
In this land good deeds are not demanded

The first perversion is hard to identify
For it leaves us feeling inwardly magnified
At ease with our choices . . . even the worst
Cheap grace feels good, but leaves us accursed

Cheap grace has a cousin
Love is her name
When she enters a discussion
She eliminates shame

She is self-evident
Expressed in a trite tautology
Love is love
Is our modern doxology

This love is free, costing nothing
It has no deep meaning
Expressed in mindless, emotional gushing
Leading the weak into daydreaming

Awaken your soul! Real love is not cheap, certainly not free
It cannot be passed off as simple and cliché
Genuine love costs more than man can perceive
A cost no one can ever truly pay

Love is love is an easy line
Conveying the emptiness of our time
But simplistic hallmark remarks
Are insufficient to guide wandering, troubled hearts

Abandon cheap love for a better desire
Voluntarily walk into the bitter fire
Seek out a love full of rich, deep meaning
And experience the wealth of your soul's own redeeming

Obedience & Belief

Only the obedient believe
Your actions reveal your axiom
Do not be deceived
Look at your life as a sum

What do you revile, what brings you shame?
Now observe your daily actions
Are these congruent . . . are they the same?

Or do your actions diverge from your stated beliefs
Do you confess words you never intend to keep
Observe in reflection what your actions admit
Stare honestly at your soul, are you a hypocrite?

And if your actions reveal a troubling pattern
Fear not, all humanity has fallen once or twice
From this experience you can learn
To follow what is right

The first step in transforming from charlatan to divine
Is to assess whether your flaw is belief or obedience
For if you obey beliefs that with evil align
Your fundamental problem is mental deviance

Observe your thought, do your beliefs rhyme
With what your conscience says?
If there is dissonance, take the time
To redirect your heart or catechize your mind

To obey is to believe
Yet belief is also obedience
It is an action rejecting deceit
Even when it is expedient

Beliefs transform the mind
Necessary to change human deeds
For you cannot expect the mentally blind
To obey good creeds

Mental clouds and deceptions
Make goodness hard to see
Truth we bend to our perception
To soothe and affirm conflicted feelings

The more beliefs we justify
To fit worldly, hedonistic desires
The harder it is to look ourselves in the eye
Instead, behind false skepticism we hide

Breaking the bonds of earthly slavery
Requires courage and divinely inspired bravery
Left to our own psychological devices
We would never resolve to pay the price

Belief and obedience share a deep connection
Correctly understood they are like a marriage
This does not meet our mental expectations
For obedience to beliefs is often disparaged

Yet observe the souls whose courage inspires
Their minds and hearts are never disconnected
Towards unity of being they aspire
To one purpose their beliefs and actions are directed

Thus, only he who believes is obedient
And only he who is obedient believes
Belief and action are interconnected ingredients
In the man who goodness, love, and grace properly perceives

The Consequence of Belief

Grace, love, belief, and obedience
Are not commodities, for they have infinite price
Grace and love are far from lenient
Instead demanding suffering and self-sacrifice

What price must man pay to seek goodness and truth?
At a minimum he must abandon the ignorance of youth
Still there is a range of possible consequence
Depending on the level of society's godlessness

Each epoch of history brings unique social conditions
Testing humanity's resolve to pursue truth and beauty
Some are blessed with healthy and happy conditions
While others are called to death as their duty

Even in cultures of contentment and peace
Some unfortunate souls are yoked with pain
Of suffering that never appears to cease
In mortal eyes, the agony may seem to be in vain

But suffering is not senseless or empty
It is a call to the ultimate prize of obedience
Those who answer the call are rewarded with eternal plenty
Even if their lives on earth are painful and tedious

For earth is a temporary space filled with strife
While death is the end, yet the beginning of life

TULIP

In the springtime flowers bloom
They arise tall and majestic
Days of wintry, dreary gloom
Give way to spring's aesthetic

In this season the Tulip unfolds
Bringing beauty to our eyes
And so in awe we now behold
The ways Tulip makes us wise

Total Depravity

The word depravity evokes a strong reaction
Instinctually from deep evil we flee
Our minds search for the nearest distraction
Fearfully, our heads turn, unwilling truth to see

Evil is an illusion; it surely does not exist
All harm is purely man-made
On this fact we collectively insist

With eyes wide shut our minds atrophy
And evil finds its foothold
Wickedness breeds agony
The delusional are easy to mold

Lust is now a godly craving
For it seeks to achieve man's pleasure
And no man is in need of saving
Instead, he should pursue his heart's treasure

Envy is no longer a fault of mortal man
Doctrine now calls for all to have the same
Across differences we constantly scan
Searching for bad identities to blame

With envy out of hiding greed soon follows
There is no room to argue here
Seeking only wealth, we become internally hollow
Desensitized to what we should hold dear

Our abundance leads to gluttony, which surely is no vice
Who are you to demand moderation?
I consume all that may entice
For there is no such thing as damnation!

Since envy has determined merit is depraved
Sloth is now seen as a virtuous manifestation
Of those society deems stunning and brave
Welcome to one of evil's many creations

Without a functioning conception of depravity
Wrath is viewed as senseless judgment
And evidence of irrationality

On this foundation pride towers over all
The narcissistic self becomes civilization's downfall

For when each individual determines what is right
Infinite clashes of will are inevitable
No two eyes will see alike
Differences of opinion become impenetrable

Pride sinks its heels in the sand
Unwilling to admit an ounce of fault
Pride issues a list of its demands
Its own image to exalt

To those outside the system the truth is plain to see
Culture eats itself when it denies total depravity

Unconditional Election

The condition of man's soul is grim and hopeless
Through his own efforts he falls into despair
Without divine intervention he can make no progress
Given his nature eternal death is entirely fair

86

Man cannot make himself attractive
He cannot create such conditions
Efforts to gain God's approval are maladaptive
Our will alone can never change our position

Restoration from the grips of self-destruction
Is a divinely granted miracle
Salvation from forms of evil's seduction
Is a departure from that which is typical

There are those who have been redeemed
Through no merit of their own
They are not what the world esteems
Making them difficult to be definitively known

The world looks to outward signs and symbols
Of wisdom, purity, and virtue
It offends our minds to be told
Sanctity is granted without our review

Mankind holds on to vice of pride, permitted he is given the chance
For this reason one man did die, serving as the condition to
     change our circumstance

Limited Atonement

In vogue is the idea that all deserve equal glory
False compassion demands men and women receive
The doctrinal version of a participation trophy
With no need for correct belief *or* good deeds

The ultimate separation of humanity
In two eternal categories
Is seen as the height of immorality
What is this cruel theology?

Limited atonement means only some partake
In the eternal life of true amazing grace

But why must this idea offend the mind?
A few moments of reflection illuminate why
All cannot dwell with the divine

The entrance of evil into human history
Could not become rendered empty
Some do not enter eternal victory
Would we prefer a gate of easy entry?

Men pine for a God they can create and control
Endlessly critiquing the divine as unkind and cruel
He is accursed for failing our circumstances to mold
Then when He punishes evil, He is viewed as brutal

Humanity desires contradictory conditions
"Give us an easy life and let us live as we choose"
Then when some are rescued to a sanctified position
The wicked cry as if another's success made them lose

In reality, all are destined to die
And no one deserves God's relation
But only the spiteful and envious would cry
When a brother or sister is spared damnation

Limited atonement is not vicious divine retribution
Rather it is a recognition of an uncomfortable certainty
Ultimately, all are subject to God's conditions
And evil must result in eternal agony

Irresistible Grace

Transformative grace is extended for free
All can access the foundation of life
No litmus test is employed, even a feeble plea
Spares a suffering soul senseless strife

Bountiful, priceless grace
Appears as a confusing mystery
What of value has no monetary stake
Is this a form of slavery?

The cost of grace cannot be calculated in currency
It asks for nothing less than the human heart
Yet with grace comes loss of social harmony
For the world threatens to tear virtue apart

Irresistible grace is attractive despite its infinite cost
Those who see its splendor were intentionally called
The chosen are aware they wander lost
Unable to fight the grace that leaves them enthralled

Earthly definitions of status, wealth, and success
Begin to feel as the yoke of the oppressed
Toiling away for human praise and affirmation
Loses its normal sense of intoxication

Grace reveals ever new depths of temptation
Pulling aside carefully crafted facades
Revealing iniquity's iteratively worse mutations
The wisest on earth know they are infinitely flawed

Asking for grace is a dangerous game
It frees the mind but brings great shame
Grace's irresistibility comes not from ease
Nor from its ability man's ego to please

It flows from the yearning for hope and beauty
The desire to seek what is holy
The longing to understand and perform one's duty
The need to live life nobly

Wandering as a pilgrim on this grim earth
May sound utterly unfashionable
Though ultimately, we return to dirt
To seek grace is the act of today's radical

Perseverance of the Saints

The presence of grace within your life
Complicates common daily affairs
Each tendency towards evil comes to light
It would be easy to fall into despair

Competing calls torment existence
Flesh commands limited attention
Perpetually you must remain resistant
To myriad forms of confusing tensions

The same grace that refines inner passion
Demands the weak man wage war
No good man is called to inaction
To conquer, sword you must draw

Not in the manner mankind expects
Violence compounds human misery
The sword of truth seeks lies to dissect
For truth ultimately breaks people free

Persevering in this endeavor brings many a danger
Without careful contemplation grace is replaced with pride
Many who seek grace to God become a stranger
Pursuing only self, evil consumes their souls till life has died

Perseverance in the face of pain is the good man's surety
He need not seek to compound suffering by chasing poverty
Pursuing holiness alone leads to earthly strife
For the world hates that which gives eternal life

RECLAIMING PRUDENCE

The tick of the clock
Brings the restless mind
To a moment of shock
"What should be done with time?"

Each day starts anew
Choices must be faced
To seek what is true
Doubt must be embraced

For over the years
Time serves as a limit
All face rational fears
Yet life has finite minutes

Diligently we seek
To find and act out truth
Doubting makes man feel weak
Thus certainty takes root

In a fast-paced world
Actions become routine
Deep thought is now obscene
Our eyes fixed on a screen

Culture breeds impatience
This flurry of action
Produces obeisance
To social factions

Prudence demands the mind pause
It is wise to heed this call
Or into error you may fall
And your mind will become small

The Gift of Time

Each life is finite, quickly dissipating
While on earth each chooses how to use time
Why live life as if in endless waiting
Indecision is one of life's gravest crimes

With a life span of roughly eighty years
Decades divide into personal history
Life's ups, downs, and inevitable tears
When properly ordered may lose mystery

Youth is designed for deep contemplation
During this time the belief system develops
At adulthood beliefs complete formation
With solid grounding the mind can accept hope

Those who enter the world adrift at sea
Powerless to articulate their beliefs
Are unable to live confidently
Ironically, they are most unfree

Sure of one belief until it costs convenience
The modern mind picks beliefs off a menu
Convinced the best ideas grant lenience
There is no longer a belief in hard truths

From life to natural death the mind is closed
Individuals possess no iron will
The ideas modern man should oppose
Are fed to him as if truth were a pill

Thus, the gift of time is snatched from modern minds
Instead of the pursuit of truth and beauty
Life becomes a quest to constantly redefine
Rendering life hopeless and void of duty

A Lost Virtue

Prudence, the ability to govern oneself
Loses meaning when choices are stripped from the mind
Why manage a life belonging not to yourself
When community rights rule each person is blind

The prudent are mocked and endlessly derided
What lay fool believes they know better than experts?
Those who attempt to use sound judgment are chided
To modern science these fools must surely convert!

Our world holds many contradictory beliefs
Licentiousness is revered; free thought disparaged
Thinking for oneself causes near endless grief
Questioning some life choices leads to outrage

True prudence in the form of discipline and reason
Are foreign to the mind of modern consciousness
Analytic abilities are now moral treason
Deep thought and reason cause the weak to feel distress

Thus, prudence is mocked; free thought is discouraged
Instead, the world makes devices our minds to distract
Wisdom is rejected; shallowness grows as we age
Universally prudence is under attack

Today's wise are hard to find, but they still exist
True to form, the prudent do not curse and whine
Their strength is quiet and easily dismissed
The vapid mind would fail to see their light shine

Yet it is the prudent that give life its purpose
For their quiet wisdom is the foundation for growth
Prudence transforms ashes of death into pure snow
Mocked and scorned, prudence remains our sure hope

Prudence & Action

Prudence must not be conflated with inaction
The prudent weigh their choices before commitment
They are not emotionally swayed by attraction
To mindless pleas they are endlessly resistant

Prudence is not mental paralysis
Some actions will inevitably be regretted
There is no such thing as perfect analysis
With soundness of mind mistakes leave us not dejected

Prudence understands the importance of context
Prudence seeks to order life according to goodness
Prudence embraces life as infinitely complex
Prudence knows the difference between change and progress

Prudence judges the wisdom of actions by context
Anger, disgust, and dark emotion have a place
Prudence is not meek or mild, leaving some perplexed
Only unthinking action does prudence hate

Prudence understands the depth of human pain
Harshness at times is the proper reaction
Pushing against evil should not be restrained
There is appropriate use of human passion

The prudent properly embody their beliefs
They understand their role in society
They study the world to process their own grief
When they choose to act, they do so decisively

When judgment is scorned prudence smiles
Such a belief is only embraced by a child
Prudence determines what is worthwhile
Judgment establishes what should be reviled

Reject the ideas supported by modern man
Act as a rebel, refuse to chain your own mind
Become prudent and through chaos you will stay sane
For prudence is the antidote to the blind

RECLAIMING MARRIAGE

"I love you" sounds cliché
For the words are easy to say
Yet beneath the surface lies a universal question
Is love purely an earthy, human deception?

What does it mean to love?
How can anyone know
The difference between affection
And a mutually beneficial transaction?

Love is unconditional, but how can this be?
Will this not readily allow
Evil men to manipulate me?
Through soft words and empty vows?

Yet, if love were fictitious, more questions arise
For without love, the soul fades . . . and dies

"Seek out experience, have fun in your youth!"
Common advice from the mouth of a culture
Where love is simply a relative truth
Ah! Countless souls have fallen prey to this vulture

Yet love and intimacy are connected
Tearing these apart comes at a cost
Many are left feeling deeply rejected
And crave enduring love not so easily lost

For love is more than a mere feeling
And it is not a social construction
Deep within love brings healing
That withstands attempts at its destruction

Counting the Costs

Will you marry me?
The question brought confusion
For I could not foresee
The relationship's conclusion

The risk was high in both directions
I could have walked away
But upon further reflection
I knew I wanted to stay

How did I know what I desired?
What put my mind at ease?
Feelings can be cunning liars
Not all desires should be appeased

The human soul is complex
Opposite desires coexisted
This knowledge my mind did vex
Until rationality persisted

Why choose the negative desires?
Why feed the beast of doubt?
When you see a pearl of infinite price
The wise secure the asset through sacrifice

Don't be a fool, you have found something rare
And you should feel no shame
In choosing commitment to visibly wear
Rather than playing a dangerous game

Evaluate the one who asked for your hand
Rather than analyzing statistics
For he is the one you must understand
Your life is not ruled by collective characteristics

Has he not shown his care for you
In deep and profound ways
Does he not voluntarily walk through
Pain your weary head to raise?

What do you seek? Society's blessing?
Or the attention of single fellas?
Social norms are often depressing
And it is not your soul that makes most men zealous

It is true your choice comes with danger
But this risk you have assumed
He could leave you and become a stranger
Yet good never grew out of irrational gloom

Your alternative is far worse
For you know he is of great worth
Instead of tossing beauty aside
Incur the small risk and become a wife

Love Is Not Blind

"Love is blind," don't marry him
For your marriage will surely fail
Signing that paper is a sin
It is your sentence to jail

Have you not seen divorce statistics?!
You are a bloody fool!
You are quite sincerely hubristic
To believe you are the exception to the rule!

You must leave him—play the field!
Or live with years of regret!
Well intentioned, they sought to shield
Me from paying an eternal debt

But lurking behind the surface
Was an attempt to win a convert
Despite shallow lip service
My free will they sought to subvert

After all, are women not free
To choose any lifestyle they please?

Yet those who supported limitless free choice
Universally scattered unsolicited advice
To one who dared to actively voice
A belief that marriage was good for her life

The judgment was swift, intense, and fierce
Determined were they my will to pierce
And so I learned to turn a blind eye
To those whose love had already withered and died

Commitment Breeds Contentment

Commitment is seen as scary
Reckless, dangerous, and daring
Its beauty and majestic glory
Hardly receive a fair hearing

Yet commitment creates positive incentives
Encouraging the cultivation of maturity
Thus creating necessary conditions
For the death of childish insecurity

In the presence of reciprocal affection
Fear and resentment fade
And the soul embraces imperfection
For another looks upon your flaws and is not afraid

Time and dedication are precious resources
When poured into the heart of another
An invisible force
Calls you to continue to discover

The infinite complexity of your spouse
For there are endless questions to learn about
The person with whom you are deeply familiar
Yet capable of leaving you confused and bewildered

Cliché and cynical advice claim two people will become bored
With just one another's company day by day
Such a view is reductionist and ill-informed
No soul is static; all humans have depths they struggle to portray

Outside the safety that loyalty breeds
We wear masks to feel at ease
Only in the shelter of eternal commitment
Can men and women find deep and abiding contentment

PURSUING HOPE

The spark that ignites the flame
Seedlings springing from dark dirt
Our hearts are dead in the ground
'Til hope whispers its first sound

What Is Hope?

Hope is by nature hard to see
Absent from earth's physical
It could be no more than a dream
Hope lives not with the cynical

When has hope fled from a soul?
What identifies despair?
With hope we need no control
Hope is a form of warfare

Hope crushes death and gives life
Hope does not manipulate
It perseveres through all strife
Our souls it does satiate

The spring of hope is for all
But some do freely reject
Another promise has called
Hope our choices does respect

Human beings each have hope
Children are always trusting
As we grow, we question hope
Much in the world is disgusting

Why does pain make us doubt hope?
Did hope promise an easy life?
Or do we simply feel lost
As if our hearts were slit by knives

Fear, anguish bring us despair
We cannot help but notice
Hope gives us a time to repair
If we listen and focus

Hope is the anchor of life
The foundation of our joy
The hopeless soul full of strife
Loves life to mock and destroy

Pay attention to dark calls
Listen to the voice of gloom
Into its snare do not fall
Or you descend into doom

Choose the path leading to life
Lest you walk through this earth blind
You will face relentless strife
While spreading hope to all mankind

Hope Is Hard

The human mind can conflate
Hope with another concept
Some can move from hope to hate
For this error all have wept

In our desire to control
We try to subjugate hope
Misunderstanding its role
Helps not our minds to cope

Hope is cheapened . . . devalued
It is now seen as a vice
Something for man to abuse
Modern wisdom is imprecise

Our minds must wrestle with hope
We must set aside the time
To grasp life beyond poor tropes
By linking our hearts and minds

Hope in man is never pure
It defies our abilities
In life all are insecure
Hope fights human frailty

The Wisdom of Hope

Wisdom . . . Discernment . . .
Traits difficult to embody
Sort between fact and fiction
Allowing hope to set us free

Hope does not tolerate lies
Hope never calls virtue vice
Hope is more than merely nice
Hope values being precise

Hope sustains us in despair
Gives us strength death to eschew
Past mistakes it can repair
Goodness Hope wants us to pursue

Hope seeks to do what is right
But before this is probable
The flesh may put up a fight
It can make life feel impossible

Hope brings more to us than joy
Hope may not be comforting
There are sad acts in our story
From death Hope is fleeing

We wrestle with Hope and pain
Condemnation strangles life
Having Hope may seem insane
Still, it overcomes our strife

Regardless of circumstance
Work hard Hope to cultivate
Never leave life up to chance
Embrace Hope your soul to elevate

Hope Assaulted

Misery and grief engulf us like a flame
From this vantage point hope is lost
Desperate and alone we are laid in shame
Sorrow and struggle leave us cross

In affliction our senses are dull and weak
Of deep anguish we dare not speak
A cloud forms before our eyes, making life dark
Without light our hearts are starved

Yearning for peace, comfort is sought despite pain
Where is hope in the darkest place?
It is *with* us when conditions cannot change
Look upward to see hope's embrace

Toil, heartache, sorrow, and destruction endure
Assaulting the being of man
Eternally hope provides security
Freeing life from darkness' hands

Hope Heals

Hope heals, it does not crush
Hope is trustworthy and kind
Hope is free of mindless mush
Instead our minds it refines

Hope is more than a feeling
Hope is a habit of trust
Hope is boundlessly freeing
Saving our souls from the dust

Hope brings awareness to pain
Preserving eyes from blindness
Whispering life is not in vain
Hope is a freeing process

THE COURAGE OF FAITH

In a robotic world, faith is a courageous choice
For it defies the assumptions on which the world turns
Vocalizing faith may cost the believer his social voice
Yet social disapproval need not leave man sullen

A culture oriented toward satisfying fleshly pleasures
Is destined to reject those who remind the collective mind
Of the dangers associated with evil's erasure
To deceived ears truth is as a picture to the blind

Since courage is hard and the modern world runs on ease
It should be no shock faith is difficult to cultivate
With attention spans begging to be constantly appeased
Pondering complex ideas is difficult to navigate

Still the faithful remain, solid and sure
Providing stability in a chaotic domain
Bearing the burden of endless mocking slurs
Determined to push against the profane

Name/Subject Index

NAME/SUBJECT INDEX

Hate/hated, 3, 36–37, 52, 56,
    58, 61, 63–65, 73, 90,
    94, 101
  hateful, 21, 60
Harm/harmed, 11, 25, 35–36,
    48, 55, 58, 60, 80,
  harmful, 37, 41, 80
Heal, 38, 74, 103
  healing, 95
Heart, 3, 27–28, 31, 37, 39, 47,
    61–63, 82–85, 89, 98,
    100, 102–3
  heartache, 29, 31, 103
Heaven, 16, 50–51
Hell, 39, 53–54, 60
History, ix, 25, 28–29, 64–65, 84,
    88, 92
Holy, 50–51, 56, 89
Hope, 3, 7–8, 14, 55, 61–63, 89,
    92–93, 100–104
  hopeless, 16, 86
  hopeful, xi
Human/humanity, x, 10, 15,
    22–24, 28–32, 35, 39–43,
    51, 56, 59, 64–67, 75,
    77–80, 82–84, 87–90,
    94–96, 99–102
  human right(s), 65, 67
  human experience/
    condition, ix, 26–27, 38
Hypocrite, 67, 82
  hypocrisy, 62

I

Ilusion, 25–26, 30–33, 85
Inclusive/inclusion, 25, 57, 63
Identity, 56, 75, 78
Independence, 25,
  independence, as in
    destroyed, 75
Indoctrinate, 75
Inferiority, 67
Insane/insanity, 7–8, 33, 61, 102
Intimacy, 3, 95

Irrational/irrationality, 3, 60–61,
    86, 97
Irresistible grace, 88–89

J

Judgment, 81, 86, 93–94, 98
Justice, 24, 44, 50, 57
Justify/justifies/justified, 39, 57,
    63–64, 81, 83
  Justification, 29, 40, 64

K

L

Law(s), 11, 30, 50, 53–54, 57, 60
Liberty, 25, 80
Lie(s), 28–29, 31, 36, 57, 60–62,
    68, 73, 90, 102
Limited atonement, 87–88
Life, 7–8, 11, 17, 23–24, 27, 41,
    48, 59, 61, 63–64, 66–68,
    84, 87–94, 100–103
Lonely/loneliness, 4, 7, 8, 10
Love/loved, 3, 26, 31–32, 42, 55,
    61–63, 66, 75, 80–82, 84,
    95, 97–98
  love is love, 81–82
  love, 'as lack of', 61
Lust, 40, 85

M

Marginalized, 55
Marxist, 49
Masculinity, 37
Mankind, 61, 87, 90, 101
Marriage/marry, 83, 95–98
Meaning, ix–x, 4, 16, 27, 35, 47,
    82, 93
Mental, 24, 26, 83
  mentally blind, 75, 83
  mental colonizers, 75
  mental illness/health, 41, 48
Mind, 4–7, 9–10, 12, 21, 23–29,
    35–36, 41, 47, 50, 53–54,

110

Vapid, 50, 93
Vengeful, 43
Vice(s), 15, 39, 40–44, 63, 86–
    87, 101–2
Victim, 33, 37, 48
Vile, 66
Violent/violence, 44, 58–59,
    64, 90
Virtue, 24–25, 40, 87, 89, 93, 102
Vision(s), 7, 51, 55
Vulnerable/vulnerability, ix,
    43–44

W
Warfare, 100
Weary, 8, 48, 96
Wise, 8, 29–30, 35, 39–40, 61,
    65, 85, 91, 93, 96
    wisdom, 27, 63, 79
    wisely, 36
    wisest, 89
Woke, 68

Woman's right, 61
Womb, 64
World, 5, 7, 10–11, 14, 16, 26–
    27, 29, 33, 35, 40, 43–44,
    51, 60, 63, 66–67, 78, 87,
    89–94, 105
    worldly, 14, 21, 33, 41, 83
    worldviews, 29
Wrath, 43–44, 86

X

Y
Yoked, 84
    yoke of the oppressed, 89
Youth, 6, 30, 57, 61, 84, 92, 95
    youthful, 54

Z

www.ingramcontent.com/pod-product-compliance
Lightning Source LLC
LaVergne TN
LVHW051647080426

835511LV00016B/2541